Common Birds
And Their Songs

Eastern Bluebird

Common Birds
And Their Songs

Lang Elliott
and Marie Read

with photos and sound recordings
by the authors and others

Houghton Mifflin Company
Boston   New York   1998

Rose-breasted Grosbeak

ISBN 0-395-91238-5

Designed and produced by Lang Elliott,
NatureSound Studio, P.O. Box 84,
Ithaca, New York 14851-0084
Typeface: Adobe Garamond; Optima

First Edition

Printed by Palace Press International Hong Kong
10 9 8 7 6 5 4 3 2 1

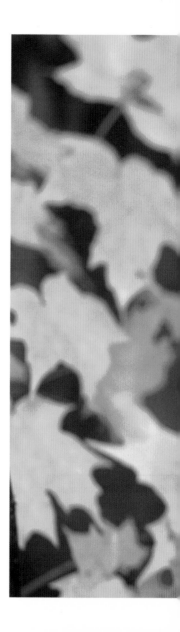

Northern Cardinal

CONTENTS

American Goldfinch

Introduction

Birds are nature's most charismatic entertainers. Clothed in brightly colored plumage, they are lively and interesting to watch. Endowed with the enviable power of flight, they are the embodiment of freedom. And, apparent to all, they perform the natural world's finest music.

Birds invite our curiosity—watching their antics we wonder why they do what they do, and we want to learn more about them. Spiritually, too, birds influence us—stirring our deepest emotions. Hearing the cries of migrating geese overhead we may feel joy, inspiration, or a profound restlessness, reminded of how unfree we humans are. Bird songs are among the finest expressions of nature's orchestra—their music lifts our spirits, celebrates each dawning day, and heralds the passing of the seasons. Whether we live in cities, suburbs, or country areas, birds are always there to greet us if we allow ourselves the time to watch and listen.

As a pastime, bird watching has ever-widening appeal. It can be enjoyed by people of all ages, in all seasons, in all places. Learning to identify birds is just the first step—a much richer appreciation of birds awaits us if we observe and study their behavior. By bird *watching,* not just bird *listing,* we gain a greater understanding of how birds interact with each other and with their environment. Looking closer at the ubiquitous American Crow, for instance, we find a clever, bold and versatile creature with a complex family life. We need never tire of the birds around us—there is something new for us to see or hear in every season.

In this beginner's guide, we introduce 50 common and widespread North American birds. Photographic close-ups, range maps, natural history text and compact disc audio are combined to convey the beauty of birds and encourage you to explore their lives. The rewards of this exploration are immense—your satisfaction guaranteed! Watching and listening to birds will help you forget your worries and will refresh your life with the spirit of the natural world. Whatever happens to you, you will never regret bringing these remarkable creatures into your life.

Bird-Watching Basics

Apart from a little free time and patience, the most basic bird-watching tool is a pair of binoculars (some bird watchers also use powerful spotting scopes, especially for viewing distant birds such as waterfowl, hawks, and shorebirds). Using binoculars takes practice at first—it's hard enough to find the bird in the lens, let alone focus on it before it flies away. Familiar birds are usually the best subjects for beginners because they are easily found, they are accustomed to people, and they often allow themselves to be observed at length.

The best place to begin is in your own backyard, your neighborhood, or in a local park. Spend ten minutes or so watching just one individual bird, perhaps a robin on your lawn or a dove on a telephone wire. Identification comes first. Note the size of the bird, its overall shape, its bill, its color pattern. Listen to its voice. Once you have determined the species, pay more attention to your subject's behavior. How does it preen, feed, and interact with other birds of the same or different species? Each species has a personality of its own that is yours to discover.

Some people complain that they have a poor memory for birds and their sounds. After several weeks of watching and listening, list the species and sounds that you recognize. You will be surprised at how many you already know. Be patient—observation is a learned skill. Study one bird at a time and your knowledge will grow faster than you think. Before long, you will suddenly realize that you are familiar with all the common birds in your surroundings—a wealth of delightful sights and sounds that greet you whenever you leave your home.

Bird Behavior

Birds spend a lot of time engaged in activities to take care of their own bodies. These *maintenance* behaviors, such as preening, bathing, and sun-basking, are necessary for the upkeep of feathers and skin. Of course, feeding, sleeping, and simply resting are also essential to a bird's well-being.

Feeding behavior provides a wealth of information about a bird, particularly about its habitat and diet. Closely tied to feeding behavior is the shape of the bill, which is adapted for collecting and processing the food types preferred by each species. For instance, herons have long, pointed bills to stab at fish. Birds that eat small mammals, such as hawks, falcons, and owls, have sharply hooked bills for tearing at flesh. In contrast, finches, grosbeaks, and other seed-eaters typically have heavy, conical bills to crush hard seeds.

Watching birds feed is an immensely pleasurable pastime that you can pursue from a lawn chair or even from your living room window. In the grass around your house, robins stalk earthworms and snatch them from the ground with lightning speed. In your garden, hummingbirds hover in front of colorful flowers, inserting their long, delicate bills to gather sweet nectar. In the trees overhead, warblers glean leaves and stems for succulent caterpillars. On tree trunks, nuthatches and woodpeckers search under bark for insects. At your bird feeder, chickadees make away with seeds. In the sky above, swallows and swifts snatch tiny insects from the air. Without a doubt, to watch a bird feed is to learn something essential about its life!

Social Behavior

Perhaps the most intriguing behaviors are the *displays* that birds perform while interacting with each other—the behaviors they use in their social lives. Technically, a display is a posture, sound, or pattern of gestures and sounds an individual produces to communicate information to a nearby recipient. Usually the recipient is a member of the same species, but it may be another species of bird or even another kind of animal. Displays are used in a wide variety of social contexts, including territory establishment and defense, courtship and nesting, and a variety of aggressive and alarm situations.

Courtship and territorial displays are extremely variable. In birds that nest gregariously, such as the Red-winged Blackbird, visual displays are elaborate and conspicuous. Grassland and open-country birds, such as the meadowlarks, often

Black-capped Chickadee

use dramatic flight displays to attract mates and define territories. In woodlands, where thick vegetation reduces visibility, inconspicuous birds such as Red-eyed Vireos and Yellow-rumped Warblers rely primarily on vocal displays to communicate vital information to mates and rivals.

Another prominent courtship behavior is *courtship feeding,* in which the female bird begs from and is fed by the male. Cedar Waxwings have a delightful *side-hop display* in which the male and female hop from side to side and pass a berry back and forth to develop and strengthen their pair bond.

Courtship behaviors take place within the framework of a species' mating system. Most songbirds are *monogamous;* one male pairs with one female for the duration of the breeding season, although "extra-pair copulations" occur in many species. Geese and swans actually mate for life, or as long as both members of the pair survive. In contrast, certain birds, such as Red-winged Blackbirds and Marsh Wrens, may be *polygynous,* with males having more than one female mate. Spotted Sandpipers are *polyandrous,* meaning that a female may mate with more than one male at a time—this is rare in the bird world. *Promiscuity* is the rule among some birds, such as the Ruffed Grouse or Wild Turkey, where males mate with any female that approaches during the breeding season.

Some birds have special antipredator displays. For instance, the Killdeer, a ground-nesting species, feigns injury with a *broken-wing display* to distract and lead a predator away from its nest. Other birds, such as mockingbirds, fly and peck at predators to drive them away. Antipredator behavior performed by a group of birds is termed *mobbing.* Dozens of crows may be seen mobbing a perched Great Horned Owl, relentlessly swooping and calling until the owl leaves the area.

During conflict at close quarters, birds often make themselves appear large and intimidating by ruffling their plumage or raising and flicking their wings. For instance, White-breasted Nuthatches have a *spread-winged aggressive display* that they use to challenge other birds, particularly at backyard bird feeders. A bird may also display aggression by stretching forward and pointing its bill at the opponent, sometimes with the bill open.

Yellow Warbler

Outside the breeding season, birds often gather in flocks. For some, flocking is closely tied to migration. Thrushes and warblers, for instance, form temporary flocks to migrate south, but tend to spread out once they reach their wintering areas. In contrast, crows, starlings, and blackbirds spend the entire winter in flocks, sometimes in huge numbers, even though they migrate only short distances or not at all. Mixed-species feeding flocks are also common, the most familar being winter assemblages of chickadees, nuthatches, and small woodpeckers, which hunt for food in each others' company.

Bird Sound

Birds communicate in many ways, and sound is one of the most important. Luckily, humans can eavesdrop on this bird conversation — songs and calls not only inform us of the presence of birds in our surroundings, they allow us to identify species and alert us to interesting behavior.

Bird sounds are perhaps best understood according to their functions. Consider the difference between what we term a *song* and a *call.* In the simplest sense, song is a loud, complex, and often musical utterance used mostly by male birds to establish and maintain a breeding territory. Calls, in contrast, are simpler and usually softer sounds used by both sexes to communicate alarm, hunger, aggression, and a variety of other motivational states.

Until recently, the word song was used primarily to describe the musical utterances produced by *songbirds,* a group famous for its members' voices (familiar songbirds include the wrens, sparrows, finches, orioles, tanagers, and warblers). However, a functional definition argues that song occurs in many other bird groups as well, including shorebirds, game birds, owls, doves, and woodpeckers. From this perspective, the musical cooing of a male Mourning Dove is functionally equivalent to the lively song of a male American Robin.

To humans, a singing performance may appear spontaneous — males perch in trees and shrubs, or fly overhead, exuberantly repeating song after song for no obvious reason. Because song is often beautiful and seemingly unprompted, we are tempted to explain its motivation in human terms: perhaps song is an expression of the joy of life. Actually song is a display. A singing male is communicating territory ownership—warning neighboring males of the same species that his territory is occupied and will be defended. While song is usually produced only by males, females of a variety of species are known to sing, although their songs are often weaker and less complex than the male's version. Singing may also advertise availability, helping unpaired males attract potential mates. And once the birds have mated, song may help maintain their pair bond.

We usually consider songs to be *vocal* sounds, produced by special organs in a bird's throat. However, certain *nonvocal* sounds can be construed as songs. Consider, for instance, the drumming of woodpeckers (produced by rapping the beak against wood) or the drumming of the grouse (produced by beating the wings). Both these signals are used during the breeding season to attract mates and define territories, and hence might be loosely classified as bird songs.

Calls, in contrast to songs, are often simple, brief sounds, like the cardinal's metallic *chip* or the robin's sharp *peek.* Many calls are subtle, being audible only at close range, and likely to be missed by the casual observer. Nonetheless, calls can be very informative. When studied in detail, most bird species are found to have a variety of different calls in their sound repertoires. Each call is usually given in a specific context or in response to a specific situation, alerting us to behavior in progress. Being able to recognize, identify, and interpret calls can tell us if aggression or courtship is occurring, if a bird is alarmed at the presence of a predator, or if a fledgling is being fed by its parents. Truly, understanding the meanings of bird calls provides us with our most intimate glimpses into birds' lives.

In this book we use the term *song* to refer to complex territorial vocalizations given mostly by males during the breeding season. Other vocalizations are referred to as *calls,* and we include their functions when known. In addition, *nonvocal* sounds are described when they play a major role in the life of a bird.

Sound Repertoires

All the auditory signals produced by a given species make up its *sound repertoire.* Some birds produce only a few sounds, while others have a greater variety of calls and song types. Scientific studies suggest that most birds use at a least a dozen different vocal displays to communicate with one another. Many of these sounds are subtle and used only at close range, during intimate communication.

Looking at song in particular, we discover that some birds, such as the Indigo Bunting and Common Yellowthroat, have one song type they repeat over and over with little variation. At the other extreme, species such as the Northern Mockingbird and the Marsh Wren may produce hundreds of different song variations. Why are there such huge differences in song repertoire size? The answer to this question is unclear, and research on this topic is ongoing.

More About Bird Song

Certain songbirds imitate the sounds of other bird species, incorporating these sounds into their songs. The Northern Mockingbird and the European Starling are well-known examples. The starling even mimics mechanical sounds and the noises of animals other than birds. Catbirds and thrashers are also imitators, as are Blue Jays, which often mimic the calls of hawks. Among birders, the ability to recognize which species these birds are imitating is a prime test of knowledge of bird sound.

Territorial disputes between male songbirds may include an interesting vocal behavior known as *countersinging,* in which neighboring males of the same species engage in song duels, singing back and forth in an alternating fashion. Northern Cardinals, Tufted Titmice, and Wood Thrushes often duel with song. A related behavior is *song-matching,* in which participants in a countersinging bout match each other's song types. The Marsh Wren is famed for this behavior.

In some species, both members of a pair may sing together in a close-knit fashion. Such *song duetting* occurs primarily in tropical birds, but some temperate-zone species show related behavior. For instance, female Brown-headed Cowbirds and female Red-winged Blackbirds often give sputtering chatters as the male sings. Duetting may help reinforce pair bonds while also sending a strong territorial message to neighbors of the same species.

More About Bird Calls

Contact calls are used between mates or among members of a flock or family group to indicate the location of the caller. In gregarious species they function in group cohesion. Such calls are often given when a bird takes flight or lands, providing important information to other birds in the vicinity.

Many birds have calls that they give primarily in flight. Eastern Bluebirds, for instance, often give a melodic *tur-a-lee* call when flying. The commonly heard flight call of the American Goldfinch sounds like *per-chik-or-ree*. Less well known are the subtle calls given during nocturnal migration flights—elusive chips and whistles made by invisible songbirds flying overhead in the dark of the night.

Alarm calls are given in situations of danger and often serve to summon the mate. They are characteristically short and sharp and tend to sound rather similar across different species. In fact, many birds pay attention to the alarm calls of other species and respond with specific behaviors. The Black-capped Chickadee offers a good example: its high warning cries given when a hawk flies overhead frequently cause nuthatches and woodpeckers, associating with the chickadees in mixed winter flocks, to freeze in place or dive for cover.

Some calls have highly specialized functions or occur only under very specific circumstances. The Eastern Phoebe, for instance, has a unique *nest-site-showing call,* which it gives while fluttering in front of a potential nest site when its mate is nearby. And the female American Goldfinch has a distinct call that she uses to solicit feeding by her mate while she is incubating the eggs on their nest.

The *begging calls* of nestlings are often shrill, repetitive sounds, which accelerate as the parent bird approaches the nest with food. After the fledglings leave the nest, their typical behavior is to crouch and vibrate their wings, all the while giving excited calls to elicit feeding.

More About Nonvocal Sounds

Nonvocal sounds used in communication are commonplace among birds. Woodpeckers rap their bills on resonant wood to produce drumming sounds that have territorial and courtship functions. Herons and owls clatter or snap their bills during aggressive or alarm situations. A male Ruffed Grouse attracts females by perching on a log and rapidly beating its wings to produce a thumping sound. Pigeons, doves, woodcock, snipe, and hummingbirds make whistling or buzzing sounds with their wings during flight and incorporate these sounds into their courtship and other displays. In fact, the more we study a bird the more likely we are to discover subtle nonvocal sounds, such as bill clicking, tapping, or feather ruffling, that are used as displays during intimate social interactions. The study of a bird's communication system is not complete until its nonvocal sounds have been investigated.

Species Accounts and Compact Disc

We've touched on the basic information that will help you understand birds and their behavior. What follows are accounts of 50 species grouped by habitat, each illustrated with a full-page photographic image. Species numbers (upper left above each bird's name) are keyed to the track numbers of the compact disc. The descriptions of the sounds reflect what is heard on the disc.

Range maps indicate summer range, year-round range, and winter range using three different colors:

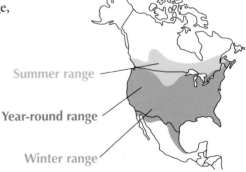

Summer range

Year-round range

Winter range

Now it's time to meet the birds!

22

Master List of Birds

Species numbers correspond to track numbers on the compact disc.

Backyard/City

1. American Robin
2. Baltimore Oriole
3. Northern Cardinal
4. Northern Mockingbird
5. Blue Jay
6. American Crow
7. Mourning Dove
8. Northern Flicker
9. Downy Woodpecker
10. House Wren
11. Black-capped Chickadee
12. White-breasted Nuthatch
13. Cedar Waxwing
14. House Finch
15. Ruby-throated Hummingbird
16. Chipping Sparrow
17. Song Sparrow
18. Evening Grosbeak

Countryside

19. Killdeer
20. Red-tailed Hawk
21. American Kestrel
22. Eastern Kingbird
23. Barn Swallow
24. Eastern Bluebird
25. Yellow Warbler
26. Indigo Bunting
27. American Goldfinch
28. Eastern Towhee
29. Eastern Meadowlark
30. Brown-headed Cowbird

Wetland

31. Canada Goose
32. Mallard
33. Wood Duck
34. Great Blue Heron
35. Belted Kingfisher

36. Tree Swallow
37. Marsh Wren
38. Common Yellowthroat
39. Red-winged Blackbird

Forest

40. Ruffed Grouse
41. Wild Turkey
42. Barred Owl
43. Great Horned Owl
44. Pileated Woodpecker
45. Wood Thrush
46. Rose-breasted Grosbeak
47. Red-eyed Vireo
48. Yellow-rumped Warbler
49. Scarlet Tanager
50. Dark-eyed Junco

American Robin
Turdus migratorius

The American Robin (10″ long) is a familiar backyard species, well known for its habit of hunting earthworms on residential lawns. When searching for a worm, a robin often tilts its head to the side to see more effectively with one eye. Territorial behavior, in which one robin runs at another with its head lowered, may also be seen on lawns. One of the earliest species to breed, the female builds a nest of coarse grasses and mud, lined with a layer of fine grasses and often placed near human habitation. Both adults feed the young, and there may be as many as three broods per year. Robins noisily attack intruders near the nest, diving and snapping their bills in response to cats and dogs or birds such as jays and crows. In fall and winter, robins form large flocks, gathering in berry-laden trees and shrubs.

Identification: Adults are dark gray above, with brick red underparts, which are darker in males. The male's head is black, the female's is gray. Juveniles resemble adults, but have heavily spotted breasts.

Habitat: Found in many environments, from dense forest to open farmland. Common in residential areas and city parks, where it frequents lawns.

Voice: The male's melodic, caroling song is a variable series of wavering, whistled phrases: *cheerily, cheeriup, cheerio, cheerily.* Short pauses occur between songs. At dawn, song may be excited and continuous, without pauses. The most common call is a high-pitched, whinnylike outburst of notes. Alarm calls given near the nest sound like *peek . . . peek . . . tut, tut . . . peek . . . tut, tut . . .*

Range: Year-round resident throughout much of the United States, although winter numbers vary in northern areas. The summer range extends north throughout most of Canada and Alaska.

Baltimore Oriole
Icterus galbula

One of the most colorful and vocal birds to be found in our backyards and gardens is the Baltimore Oriole (8″ long). Orioles nest in large shade trees, weaving their distinctive pendulous, socklike nests at the tips of drooping branches. They search about in trees and shrubs for caterpillars and other insects and also eat fruit. Both male and female sing. The Baltimore Oriole and its western counterpart, the Bullock's Oriole, until recently were considered subspecies of a single wide-ranging species, the Northern Oriole.

female

Identification: The breeding male has bright orange underparts and rump, with black upperparts, head, and throat and white wing bars. The female is olive-green above, dull yellow-orange below. Bullock's Oriole males differ by having orange cheeks, black cap and throat, and bold white wing patches.

Habitat: Open woodlands, riverine woodlands, orchards, parks, and gardens with shade trees. Easily attracted to bird feeders with fruit, peanut butter, or cornmeal-fat mixes.

Voice: Song is a sequence of bright, slurred whistles, sometimes with prominent harsh or raspy notes. Both sexes sing, although female song is usually simpler in pattern. Songs of individual birds vary considerably, but each sings a characteristic, recognizable song pattern. Single whistled notes function as contact calls. Common calls include a nasal *jeet-jeet* and a rattling chatter. Fledglings make loud nasal calls sounding like *dee-dee-dee.*

Range: Summers throughout the eastern United States. Winters in Florida and the Gulf Coast, into Central America.

Northern Mockingbird
Mimus polyglottos

As its Latin name suggests, the Northern Mockingbird (10″ long) is a renowned vocal mimic, imitating other birds' songs and various other sounds. Aggressively territorial, the male mockingbird claims a breeding territory in spring, chasing intruders and displaying at them with wings raised and tail wagging up and down. To attract a mate he sings loudly and performs looping flight displays to and from a conspicuous perch. At first he may chase the female, but soon he accepts her. Both adults build the nest and defend the young from approaching predators, boldly swooping at dogs, cats, large birds, snakes, and humans. In autumn, male and female each sing and defend separate feeding territories, usually centered around a berry-covered tree or shrub, where they chase fruit-eating competitors including robins, starlings, jays, and other mockingbirds.

Identification: Adults of both sexes are gray above and whitish below, with blackish wings and tail. White outer tail feathers and bold wing patches are striking in flight and during displays.

Habitat: Woodland edges, rural and suburban thickets, farms, towns.

Voice: The song is a long-continued stream of loud phrases, many being imitations of other birds' songs and calls along with the sounds of squeaky gates, machinery, barking dogs, and humans whistling. Each song phrase is repeated three or more times before changing to the next. Males sing in spring, and both sexes sing in fall, although female song is usually quieter. Mockingbirds often sing at night. Common calls include a raspy *chjjjjj* and a harsh *chewk*.

Range: Year-round resident throughout most of the United States. Appears to be expanding its range north, especially in the Northeast.

Blue Jay
Cyanocitta cristata

Conspicuous, bold, and gregarious, the Blue Jay (12″ long) is a familiar but often unwelcome visitor to backyard bird feeders, where its rowdy flocks displace less assertive species. Nonetheless, jay social behavior is fascinating to watch. During spring courtship, noisy males hop and fly around females, calling loudly and performing a vigorous bobbing display whenever they land. After pairing, jays are much quieter as they secretly search for a nest site. However, once the nest is built, the pair loudly mobs predators that come too close. In fall, Blue Jays gather into foraging flocks. They often cache food, filling their expandable throat pouches with seeds or nuts, then flying off to hide them under bark or in a tree crevice, to be used later as a winter food source.

Identification: Both male and female have blue upperparts, grayish white underparts, a striking black collar and necklace, and a blue crest. Wings and tail are spotted with white and have wide black bars.

Habitat: Woodlands, parks, suburbs, often at backyard feeders.

Voice: The common call is a harsh, jeering *jaay* or *jaay-jaay,* which often attracts other jays. Intense versions are given in alarm. Calls accompanying the bobbing display include a musical, bell-like *toolool, toolool,* a squeaky *wheedleee, wheedelee,* and odd clicking sounds. Soft nasal notes are given when birds are in close proximity, especially during mate feeding and nest building. Blue Jays frequently mimic hawk calls, especially those of the Red-shouldered Hawk.

Range: Year-round resident across central and eastern United States and much of southern Canada.

6

American Crow
Corvus brachyrhynchos

Adaptable and intelligent, the American Crow (18″ long) is a highly communicative bird with a complex social life. The breeding pair may be assisted by their grown offspring from previous years, who share all nesting activities and help raise the nestlings (their own siblings). Crows loudly mob hawks, owls, and mammalian predators. They spend fall and winter in large flocks, gathering in food-rich areas, then flying at dusk to communal roosts. Well adapted to living near humans, urban crows feed on garbage and road-killed animals. Rural crows feed on grain, insects, earthworms, the eggs of other birds, and anything else that is edible.

Identification: A large, all-black bird with a long, heavy bill. In flight, its rounded tail distinguishes the American Crow from the Common Raven, a larger bird with a wedge-shaped tail.

Habitat: Frequents a wide variety of semi-open habitats, from urban areas to agricultural regions.

Voice: The crow's familiar *caw, caw* has many subtle variations whose meanings are poorly understood. Long notes, repeated raucously for several minutes, seem to be assembly calls. Excited, higher-pitched calls signify alarm. Phrases of three or four *caws* may be used as contact calls. Calling is often accompanied by visual displays, including bobbing the head up and down rhythmically or flicking the tail. Begging fledglings give a nasal *cah* and various gagging sounds. Other crow vocalizations include rattling, gurgling, and cooing notes.

Range: Year-round resident throughout most of the United States except for scattered areas in the Southwest. Summer range includes subarctic Canada.

7

Mourning Dove
Zenaida macroura

Our commonest and most widespread native dove, the Mourning Dove (12″ long) often visits backyard bird feeders. Its natural food includes a variety of seeds, grains, and insects. To attract a mate, the perched male gives a melancholy cooing call while puffing out his throat and bobbing his tail. More dramatic is the male's aerial display, in which he takes flight with a noisy clapping of wings and then flies high into the sky before gliding downward in a long spiral. During courtship, the cooing male struts and bows repeatedly in front of the female. As in other pigeons and doves, nestlings are fed a nutritious white liquid known as "pigeon milk," which is regurgitated by the parents.

Identification: Adults are sleek gray-brown overall, with black spots on the wings and a pinkish brown wash on the underparts. The long tail tapers to a point. The male has subtle iridescence on the sides of his neck and a grayish crown.

Habitat: Frequents a wide variety of open habitats, including farmyards, fields, suburban areas, and backyards.

Voice: The male's territorial and courtship call is a series of mournful cooing notes, with the second note stressed and higher in pitch than the others: *oo-wah-hoo-oo-oo.* This call may be mistaken for the hooting of a distant owl. A shorter call, *oo-waoh,* is used by both sexes during activities near the nest. Mourning Doves often produce a prominent whistling twitter when flying, especially during takeoff or landing. This nonvocal sound may indicate alarm.

Range: Year-round resident across the United States except for the northern Great Plains region. Summer range extends into southern Canada.

8

Northern Flicker
Colaptes auratus

Of all our woodpeckers, the common and widespread Northern Flicker (12″ long) is the most conspicuous and the most likely to be seen on the ground, where it feeds on ants and beetle larvae. Its loud calls and drumming advertise its presence during the spring and summer breeding season. The flicker's nest is a cavity in a large tree, excavated mostly by the male. Two forms exist, which were once considered separate species — the yellow-shafted in the East and the red-shafted in the West.

Identification: Adults of both sexes have brown-barred backs, white rumps, and spotted underparts with a black crescent-shaped bib. Yellow-shafted males (see photograph) have a black mustache, whereas red-shafted males have a red mustache. Females of both forms lack the mustache. Underwings of yellow-shafted flickers are yellow; those of red-shafted are red.

Habitat: Open woodlands, suburban areas. Often feeds on lawns.

Voice: The flicker's most obvious call is a loud, rapid sequence of notes, *ki-ki-ki-ki-ki-ki-ki*, used for territory advertisement, mate attraction, and maintaining the pair bond. Another common call is an abrupt, down-slurred *peeough* used as a contact call between mates or members of a family group. A repeated *flicka-flicka-flicka-flicka* occurs during encounters, both aggressive and courtship, and is often accompanied by pointing the bill upward. Courtship displays include lively head-bobbing and weaving. Flickers also drum with their bills on resonant wood, particularly on their chosen nest tree.

Range: Year-round resident throughout the continental United States. Summer range extends into northern Canada and Alaska. Northern populations migrate.

9

Downy Woodpecker
Picoides pubescens

The persistent drumming of the Downy Woodpecker (6″ long) is a welcome sign that winter will soon come to an end. In mid-winter, members of a pair have overlapping territories but lead separate lives. In late winter, they begin to coordinate their activities, each drumming from one of several favorite trees. When spring finally arrives, territorial and courtship behaviors increase, and one can observe displays directed toward the prospective mate or intruders, with bill waving, wing raising, and chasing up trees and in flight, all accompanied by loud calls. The nest is a cavity in a rotten tree, created primarily by the male.

Hairy Woodpecker

Identification: Downy Woodpeckers of both sexes have white backs and underparts and black wings with white spots. Their bold black-and-white facial patterns vary and can be used to identify individuals. Males have a red nape patch, females have no patch. The ratio of bill length to head width is used to distinguish the Downy Woodpecker from the larger Hairy Woodpecker: Downy bill length is about half the head width, whereas Hairy bill length approximately equals head width.

Habitat: Open and dense woodlands, farmland, suburbs. Visits suet feeders.

Voice: Familiar calls include a sharp *peek!* and a high-pitched, descending whinny. An excited *queek-queek-queek* is given during courtship. Both sexes drum on resonant wood, producing a rapid outburst lasting about a second.

Range: Year-round resident throughout the United States (except for scattered areas in the Southwest) and much of subarctic Canada.

10

House Wren
Troglodytes aedon

"A plain little bird with a loud, exuberant song and busy ways" aptly describes the House Wren (5″ long). Males claim their territories in spring by singing boldly from prominent perches and placing small sticks as nest foundations in several potential nest cavities (either tree holes or nest boxes). When a female arrives, the courting male sings excitedly, with trembling wings. Once paired, he leads her to each nest site, flying ahead of her with distinctive fluttering wingbeats. After choosing her favorite nest cavity, the female adds a lining of grasses, hair, and feathers to the male's base of sticks. Females often have two broods each season and may pair with another male for the second brood. House Wrens forage on the ground and in vegetation for insects and spiders.

Identification: A small bird with finely barred, brown upperparts and buffy underparts. The short, rufous-brown tail is often held cocked. The sexes look alike.

Habitat: Common and abundant in rural and suburban areas—prefers woodland edges, brushy habitats, orchards, farmyards, and parks.

Voice: The male's song is a rich, bubbling chatter. It starts slowly, rises in volume and pitch, then drops, ending with a rapid cascade of notes. During courtship, song is more excited and includes many harsh, squeaky notes. Loud churring rattles are given in alarm, especially when there is danger to the young. Other sounds include buzzing notes and simple *chit* calls used in a variety of situations.

Range: Summers across the United States, except the Gulf states, and into southern Canada. Winters across most of the southern states. Resident year-round in the extreme Southwest and through Mexico.

11

Black-capped Chickadee
Poecile atricapillus

The tame and lively Black-capped Chickadee (5″ long) forages acrobatically through branches, sometimes hanging upside down to glean insects, seeds, and berries, or briefly hovering to drink tree sap. At backyard feeders it opens sunflower seeds by holding them in its feet and cracking them with its bill. In winter, chickadees form structured, stable flocks that defend a feeding territory. Nuthatches, titmice, and woodpeckers often join them, forming a mixed-species foraging flock. In late winter, chickadee flocks begin to break up, and males start singing and becoming more territorial. As breeding season approaches, females solicit mate feeding. Chickadees breed in nest boxes or excavate nest holes in rotting tree stumps, carrying out wood chips in their bills.

Carolina Chickadee

Identification: Gray upperparts, lighter underparts, a black cap and bib, and white feather edges on wings. The sexes are alike. The Carolina Chickadee of the southern states looks much like the black-capped, but lacks white edges on the wings.

Habitat: Open woods, farmland, suburbs, city parks, backyards.

Voice: The song of the male is a clear two-note whistle that drops in pitch: *fee-beeee* (the last note is often double-pulsed). The familiar *chicka-dee-dee-dee* call, after which the species is named, is given during flocking and helps insure flock cohesion. A gargled *tseedleedeet* is given during aggressive encounters. Other calls include a simple *tsit* (the contact note) and various outbursts of notes.

Range: Year-round resident throughout the northern half of the United States and much of subarctic Canada.

12

White-breasted Nuthatch
Sitta carolinensis

The White-breasted Nuthatch (6″ long) is most often seen scurrying jerkily down a tree trunk headfirst, foraging for insects. Diet also includes various nuts and seeds, any of which it may store in crevices for future use. At feeders it enjoys sunflower seeds and suet, aggressively keeping other birds at bay with a dramatic display—swaying from side to side with wings outspread. Nuthatch pairs remain on their territories after breeding, but interact little until late winter, when courtship resumes. The male sings from an exposed perch. When the female approaches, he displays by bowing with each note. As courtship progresses, mate feeding becomes frequent. The nest is placed in a tree hole. In winter, nuthatches often forage in small flocks alongside chickadees, creepers, and woodpeckers.

Identification: Adults have blue-gray backs, whitish faces and underparts, and varying amounts of chestnut on the flanks. In areas other than the Southeast, crown and nape color can distinguish the sexes, being glossy black in males and gray or dull black in females.

Habitat: Deciduous and mixed woodlands, backyard feeders.

Voice: The male's song is a vibrant series of nasal notes sounding like *hey-hey-hey-hey-hey.* Song may be heard from midwinter through spring. The common call is a loud, nasal *ank,* given either singly, in pairs, or in a rapid series that indicates alarm or excitement. Soft *ip* or *ik* notes are used as intimate contact calls by nuthatches as they move around together.

Range: Resident year-round throughout the United States, excluding Florida, part of Texas, and western desert regions.

13

Cedar Waxwing
Bombycilla cedrorum

The Cedar Waxwing (7″ long) is gregarious year-round, feeding in flocks even during the breeding season. Sugary fruit is the primary diet, although waxwings also catch insects while flying, especially over water. Courtship includes a ritual in which the male and female hop from side to side and pass a fruit, insect, or flower petal back and forth until the female finally eats it. Nesting occurs in late summer; the young are fed fruit. Waxwings winter in large flocks and roam widely in search of food. A flock can strip a berry-laden tree of fruit in a day or two. In late winter, waxwings often eat fermented berries and become intoxicated.

Identification: Adults of both sexes have silky buff-brown plumage, sleek crests, black facial masks, and yellow-tipped tails. Red waxy tips on the secondary wing-feathers give the waxwing its name but are not always present; they are thought to signal age or social status. Juvenile plumage is streaky, and young birds lack the facial mask.

Habitat: Woodlands, orchards, open areas with berry-bearing shrubs and trees. Often seen near water. Nomadic in winter.

Voice: Adults of both sexes make a high-pitched, hissy whistle, *seeeeeeee,* most often given in flight or when taking off. A high buzzy trill, *bzeeeeee,* is the most common call given by perched waxwings. Begging juveniles and females during courtship give rapid sequences of these trills: *bzeee-bzeee-bzeee-bzeee . . .*

Range: Year-round resident through much of central and northern United States. Summer range extends across southern Canada. Winters in the southern United States, Mexico, and Central America.

14

House Finch
Carpodacus mexicanus

Originally from the West, captive House Finches (5½″ long) were released by pet-shop owners in New York City in 1940. Now the species is a common resident throughout the East in urban and suburban areas. Its spread is thought to have been helped by the popularity of backyard bird feeders. Natural foods include weed seeds, plant buds, and fruit. During courtship, the singing male hops and flutters around the female, who may also sing briefly. Well adapted to the human environment, the House Finch often builds its nest in shrubbery close to houses or in hanging planters. It is a sociable species, forming small flocks in winter.

female

Identification: The male has gray-brown upperparts, with broad brownish streaking on the belly and flanks and red on the head, breast, and rump (in some regions the red is replaced by orange or yellow). The female is uniformly gray-brown above, with brownish-streaked underparts.

Habitat: Urban and suburban areas, parks. In the West, habitat also includes semi-arid regions and canyons.

Voice: Song is a cheery, musical warble lasting several seconds, often ending with a harsh, descending note. In the presence of a female, males may sing an excited, more continuous version. Females occasionally sing simplified songs. A common call is a nasal *wheet* or *seet,* sometimes given sharply, other times in a more drawn-out manner. Another distinctive call sounds like *chi-chuwee.*

Range: Year-round resident throughout the western United States, Mexico, and much of the East (except Florida); absent from the central states. Range expanding.

15

Ruby-throated Hummingbird
Archilochus colubris

With jewellike colors and whirring wings, the Ruby-throated Hummingbird (3¾″ long) zips from flower to flower, hovering to sip nectar. Despite its tiny size, it belligerently defends food sources in its territory, chasing off other hummingbirds, bees, and nectar-feeding sphinx moths. Courtship and territorial behavior include a spectacular "pendulum arc display," in which the male swings back and forth in a U-shaped arc, rising high into the air on each side. Ruby-throated Hummingbirds do not form pairs; the male and female meet just for mating, then the female nests and raises the young alone. The tiny nest is built of lichens, plant scales, and fluff, bound together with spider webs; it resembles a mossy knot on a tree limb. Young Ruby-throats are fed insects as well as nectar.

female

Identification: The adult male has glossy green upperparts, whitish underparts, and an iridescent red throat, which appears black under some lighting conditions. The female is similar, but lacks the colorful throat.

Habitat: Woodland edges, parks, gardens. A common visitor to backyard hummingbird feeders.

Voice: Ruby-throats give both vocal and nonvocal sounds. The common call is a squeaky *chit* or *chitit,* given during interactions and accompanied by wing hum. More complex calls occur during aggressive chases. The pendulum arc display is accompanied by buzzy wing hum and high-pitched twittering.

Range: Summer visitor only, breeding throughout the eastern United States and across southern Canada except the Far West. Winters in Central America.

16

Chipping Sparrow
Spizella passerina

In the era of horse-drawn carriages, the Chipping Sparrow (5½″ long) was sometimes referred to as the "hair bird," for its habit of lining its nest with horsehair. Indeed, this bird has benefited greatly from human activities. Originally a species of open pine woodlands, it is now one of our commonest backyard sparrows and frequently chooses to nest in ornamental evergreen shrubs planted around building foundations. The male sings in spring from a prominent perch in his territory. Neighboring males have distinctive song patterns that can be individually recognized. During territorial encounters, a resident male will threaten an intruder with drooped wings before chasing his adversary from the area. In fall and winter, Chipping Sparrows form small flocks, often with other sparrows and juncos.

Identification: In breeding plumage, adults of both sexes have streaked brown backs, light gray breasts with no markings, bright rufous-brown caps, and a strong black line through the eye. In winter, adult head markings are less distinct, the crown being more streaked.

Habitat: Widely distributed. Prefers grassy areas, open woodlands, parks, suburbs, and backyards. Common visitor to bird feeders.

Voice: The male's typical song is a rapid series of dry chips lasting several seconds. At dawn, males sing shorter songs in a more lively sequence, often perching on or near the ground. Calls include a high-pitched *chip* and a more drawn-out *seet*.

Range: Summers throughout the United States and subarctic Canada. Year-round resident from the southern states into Mexico and Central America. Wintering populations found in Florida, Texas, and Mexico.

17

Song Sparrow
Melospiza melodia

As its name suggests, the Song Sparrow (6″ long) is well known for its melodious voice. Early in spring, males spend long periods each day singing conspicuously from favored perches. They threaten intruding males by fluffing out their feathers, waving one or both wings while singing, and then chasing the rival if he persists. Courtship behavior involves the male swooping down at the perched female, who responds by giving a trilling call. Once paired, Song Sparrows stop singing and become secretive. The well-hidden nest is built by the female on or near the ground in thick vegetation.

Identification: The Song Sparrow population consists of many subspecies that vary in size and coloration. In general, adults have brown streaked upperparts and whitish underparts with streaks on sides and breast that often converge to form a distinctive central spot.

Habitat: Dense shrubbery at edges of fields, backyard lawns, streamside thickets, and marsh edges. Visits bird feeders.

Voice: The male's song begins with several bright notes followed by a sequence of warbles and trills that varies considerably among individuals. Each male has a repertoire of up to ten different song types and repeats one type several times before switching to another. Although songs vary, the species pattern is easy to learn and recognize. When agitated, Song Sparrows give a nasal *chimp* or a high-pitched *tsip*.

Range: Year-round resident through most of northern half of United States, including the entire West Coast north to Alaska. Summer range extends across much of Canada. Northern birds migrate south to the southern United States or Mexico.

18

Evening Grosbeak
Coccothraustes vespertinus

Its massive bill tells us that the Evening Grosbeak (8″ long) feeds primarily on seeds. Pine and box elder seeds are favorites, but the grosbeak diet also includes fruit, buds, and insects. The species breeds in northern forests and mountainous areas, building a skimpy nest high in a conifer tree. Grosbeaks are unpredictable winter visitors to our feeders. In some years they descend in large noisy flocks to devour sunflower seeds; in other years they stay in northern areas and are absent from much of their potential winter range. Large-scale southern movements are termed "irruptions" and are thought to result from winter food shortages in northern areas, such as the periodic failure of pine cone crops. When courting, a male dances in front of a prospective mate with his wings drooped and vibrating.

Identification: Adult male has a yellow body, dark head, and a yellow forehead and eyebrow. Female is brownish gray overall. Adults of both sexes have black-and-white wings, and their bills change from pale yellow in winter to greenish in summer.

Habitat: Breeds in northern woodlands, especially among conifers. Winter habitat includes a variety of open areas with trees and shrubs. Visits backyard feeders.

Voice: The most familiar call is a loud, ringing *peeeer* or *chee-yer,* given when perched and in flight. Also gives soft, throaty trills. Its warbling song is rarely heard.

Range: Year-round resident across southern Canada, northernmost regions of New England, and northwestern United States. Southern year-round range is limited to the Rocky Mountain region, extending south to northern Mexico. Winter range includes most of the United States, excluding the Gulf Coast and Florida, but is highly variable from year to year.

19

Killdeer
Charadrius vociferus

A shorebird that has adapted to life in many suburban and agricultural settings, the Killdeer (10″ long) is named for its distinctive ringing calls. The species is well known for its dramatic predator-distraction display, in which it feigns injury, dragging its tail and fluttering its wing as if broken, all the while calling plaintively and leading intruders away from the nest or young. The well-camouflaged eggs are laid in a simple scrape on barren ground.

Identification: Both sexes are brown above and white below, with a distinctive red-orange eye ring and two black bands around the neck. The reddish brown rump is most visible in flight or when a bird displays. Immature birds resemble adults, with buffy tips on their back and wing feathers.

Habitat: Found in suburban and rural areas, where it favors open ground with gravel and the short, sparse vegetation of athletic fields, agricultural areas, and residential lawns. Often nests on gravel driveways and rooftops. Also seen feeding on lake shores and mudflats, especially during migration.

Voice: The best-known call is a loud *kill-dee, kill-dee, kill-dee,* given as males perform wide circle-flights over their territories in early spring. Plaintive nasal alarm calls sound like *k'dee . . . k'dee . . . k'dee-dee-dee,* or a repeated *deet-deet-deet-deet.* Another distinctive call is a long stuttering trill, which may accompany courtship, aggressive encounters, and alarm situations.

Range: Resident year-round in the southern half of the United States and throughout the West. Summer range extends from the northern states to subarctic Canada and southern Alaska. Winters in Mexico and Central America.

20

Red-tailed Hawk

Buteo jamaicensis

On clear days, when the sun's warmth creates thermal uplifts, the Red-tailed Hawk (19″–25″ long) may be seen soaring against the blue sky. Its aerial prowess figures prominently in hunting for food, in territorial defense, and in courtship behavior. Circling high over its territory, the Red-tail easily locates hawk intruders. Territorial interactions in flight include swooping and diving down upon the adversary with talons extended. Courtship behavior looks similar, with the pair soaring close together, sometimes appearing to touch, and giving loud screams and chirping calls. Both mates build the nest or renovate an old one, often lining it with green sprigs of coniferous vegetation, which may deter feather parasites.

Identification: Plumage is highly variable, especially in the West. Adults of both sexes are usually brown above, with light underparts, sometimes with a dark belly band. The upper surface of the adult's tail is distinctly brownish red. Immatures generally have heavily streaked or spotted underparts and gray-brown tails barred with many narrow stripes.

Habitat: Open country, plains, prairies, woodland edges, mountains, and deserts.

Voice: The familiar call of perched or flying birds is a shrill, down-slurred, hissy scream, *tseeeeeeaarr,* directed at intruding hawks and humans, or given during courtship. This call is the familiar "eagle scream" heard in movies. An up-slurred, chirping *klooeek, klooeek* is given by courting adults, often during aerial courtship displays, and also by fledglings.

Range: Year-round resident throughout United States except for the northernmost areas of the Midwest. Summer range extends across Canada to Alaska.

21

American Kestrel
Falco sparverius

Often seen hovering over fields and open areas, the American Kestrel (9″ long) is one of our most active and colorful birds of prey. It captures insects, reptiles, and mice by suddenly diving from midair. The nest site is a natural tree cavity or cliff nook, an old woodpecker hole, or a nest box. Soon after pairing but before egg laying, the female kestrel stops hunting and relies on her mate to bring her food until one or two weeks after the young have hatched. During mate feeding, the male arrives with conspicuous whining calls and lands at the pair's food-transfer perch. The female joins him and both display with bobbing heads. The female then takes the food to another perch to eat it, stores it, or feeds it to the young. As the young grow, both parents must hunt for food to keep them satisfied.

Identification: Adult male has rufous-brown back, blue-gray wings, and a rufous tail with a dark band at the tip. Adult female is mostly rufous-brown, with bars on the back and tail and streaked underparts. Both sexes have a pair of vertical black stripes on the face. Young kestrels resemble adults.

Habitat: Open country, agricultural areas, woodland edges, and cities.

Voice: The most familiar call is a series of sharp metallic notes, *klee-klee-klee-klee,* given when alarmed and during territorial and courtship interactions. Both male and female make plaintive, whining calls during mate feeding; begging fledglings give similar calls.

Range: Year-round resident throughout most of the United States. Summer range extends over much of Canada to Alaska. Winters from southern Texas into Mexico and Central America.

22

Eastern Kingbird
Tyrannus tyrannus

The Eastern Kingbird (9″ long) exemplifies its family's common name of "tyrant flycatchers" by being aggressively territorial and boldly attacking larger birds such as crows and hawks, even if they are high in the air above the nest. Highly vocal throughout the breeding season, paired kingbirds perform a greeting display whenever they meet, fluttering their wings and calling noisily.
The untidy nest is often in an exposed location, sitting atop a fence post or tree stump or at the end of a branch, very often over water. The male stands guard near the nest when the incubating female leaves to feed, but she allows his close approach only when the young hatch. Both parents then feed the young. Like other flycatchers, Eastern Kingbirds feed by darting out from a perch to capture flying insects.

Identification: Adults of both sexes have slate gray upperparts and whitish underparts, with a prominent white band at the very end of the tail. A concealed orange-red crown patch is seldom seen.

Habitat: Woodland edges, river edges, farms, orchards, roadsides, and hedgerows. Often seen perching on fences and wires and near water.

Voice: Males sing at the break of dawn and sometimes at dusk, giving a complex series of stuttering, high-pitched notes sounding like *t-t-t’t’t’-tzeet-tzeeert,* repeated time and again. Common calls include a high, buzzy *ktzee* and a ringing *ktseet.* A rapid outburst of high notes known as the "kitter call" is given as a greeting call when members of a family come together: *kitter-kitter-kitter-kitter.*

Range: Summer visitor only, breeding throughout much of the United States and southern Canada.

23

Barn Swallow
Hirundo rustica

The Barn Swallow (7″ long), recognized by its long forked tail, is a species that benefits from human activities, locating its nest on ledges and walls of barns and other buildings or under bridges and docks. Pairs typically nest close together, forming loose colonies. Barn Swallows seldom perch on the ground, except when gathering mud with their beaks for building nests. Adapted for life on the wing, they capture flying insects, often swooping low over water to snatch prey from the surface and to drink. In late summer, adults and fledglings gather into lively twittering flocks, often perching on telephone wires, as they prepare for their migration to southern wintering areas.

Identification: Slender-bodied birds with long pointed wings. Adults have blue-black upperparts and buffy underparts with reddish brown chin and throat. The tail is deeply forked in adults, shorter but still noticeably forked in juveniles.

Habitat: Open country, especially near farms, often found near water.

Voice: The typical male song is a short series of twittering notes followed by a melodic, gurgling jumble. During the courtship phase, swallows may perch together on a telephone wire or roof ridge or circle about in the air, calling and singing noisily. At dawn, solitary males often sing a prolonged, continuous series of squeaky twitters, perched or when flying over the nesting area. Alarm calls include a metallic *chi-deep* and a staccato *chit*. Begging young give repeated, raspy calls from the nest.

Range: The Barn Swallow is a summer resident only, its breeding range extending across the United States (except the extreme Southeast) and much of subarctic Canada. Winters from Central America to South America.

24

Eastern Bluebird
Sialia sialis

Recent conservation efforts to set up nest boxes have helped the beautiful Eastern Bluebird (7″ long) recover from a population decline that began early this century. Introduced species such as the European Starling and the House Sparrow compete with the bluebird for tree holes, which are its traditional nest sites, and which, because of deforestation, are now in short supply. During courtship, the male sings and displays by performing a butterfly-like flight and hovering outside potential nest sites. When the female approaches, the male gives a wing-waving display. Bluebirds feed on ground-living insects, which the birds locate while perched. They form small flocks in winter, when their diet also includes berries.

female

Identification: Adult male has deep blue upperparts; female has grayish upperparts with a blue wash, deeper on the wings and tail. Both adults have chestnut throats and chests and whitish bellies. Immatures resemble the adult female, but with gray-brown spotted breasts. The species' western counterpart, the Western Bluebird, looks similar, but the male's upperparts and throat are deep purple-blue.

Habitat: Farmlands, mature orchards, and open woodlands.

Voice: The song, given mainly by the male, is a series of melodious, gurgling whistles sometimes sounding like *cheer, cheer, cheerful, charmer.* A sweet *tur-a-lee* is a commonly heard contact call often given in flight. Agitated chattering signifies alarm.

Range: Year-round resident across the southern half of the eastern United States and the Northeast. Summer range includes the Midwest and southeastern Canada.

25

Yellow Warbler
Dendroica petechia

One of the most familiar and conspicuous spring warblers, the Yellow Warbler (5″ long) is easily recognized by its canary yellow coloration and its bright, cheery song. It gleans most of its insect food from vegetation, but may perform short circle-flights to capture insects on the wing. The dense cup-like nest, built by the female in a low shrub, is constructed of fine plant fibers and fluffy down from willow and poplar seeds, held together with webbing from tent caterpillar nests. Nests are often parasitized by Brown-headed Cowbirds; the warblers may respond by covering the cowbird eggs with additional nest material and then laying a new clutch.

Identification: In breeding plumage both sexes have overall yellow plumage with yellow-olive back, wings, and tail. The male has distinct rusty-red streaks on breast and belly; in females these are faint or absent.

Habitat: Inhabits thickets associated with wet areas, especially willow and alder clumps along streams and lakes. Also found in woodlands, gardens, and orchards, especially where there is shrubby or brushy cover.

Voice: The male's song, often given from a high, exposed perch, is a bright, clear *see-see-see-titi-see,* for which there is a well-known memory phrase: "sweet, sweet, sweet, sweet-than-sweet!" Males have one predominant song pattern that they sing during most of the day. However, at dawn and during aggressive encounters, males sing a variety of other song types, often changing type with each new song. The common alarm call is a musical *chip.*

Range: Summers throughout most of North America except for the Gulf states. Year-round resident in Mexico and Central America.

26

Indigo Bunting
Passerina cyanea

Vivid blue plumage and a clear whistled song make the Indigo Bunting (5½″ long) one of the delights of a summer day. The male is conspicuous in appearance and habit, singing loudly from high treetops within his territory. During territorial encounters, he may perform a fluttering display flight with fluffed body feathers and outspread wings and tail. Unlike her mate, the female Indigo Bunting is subdued in color and secretive in behavior. Her nest, hidden in a low shrub, is one of the most difficult to find. The sexes lead somewhat separate lives after mating. The male rarely visits the nest and plays little part in raising the young, but he does act as a guard against possible danger.

Identification: Adult male in breeding plumage is deep blue overall. Winter male is brownish with some blue on underparts, wings, and rump. Adult female is plain brown overall, with faint streaking on the breast. Immature males in fall resemble adult female; by their first summer their plumage becomes a mix of brown and blue feathers, becoming entirely blue in their second summer.

Habitat: Open areas with shrubbery and low trees, such as overgrown fields, pastures, and woodland clearings.

Voice: The male's lively song is composed of variable, high-pitched whistled notes, most of them paired: *see-see, zeet-zeet, chit-chit, seeit-seetz.* A bubbly version of song accompanies flight displays. Sharp *chip* calls are given in alarm situations.

Range: Summer visitor only, breeding throughout the eastern half of the United States and scattered areas in the Southwest. Winters mainly in Central America, with some individuals wintering in southern Florida.

27

American Goldfinch
Carduelis tristis

The American Goldfinch (5″ long) is a common gregarious species, well known for its bright plumage, undulating flight, and
tinkling calls. In fall and winter small flocks feed on seeds, particularly of thistles, dandelions, and sunflowers. Some courtship
behavior occurs in spring, but nesting is delayed until late summer,
and young are fed mostly on seeds. The nest is densely woven of plant
fibers, strengthened with spider or caterpillar web and lined with thistledown. The
female incubates the eggs almost continuously, receiving food brought by the male.

female

Identification: Male in breeding plumage is bright yellow with
black wings, tail, and cap. Female is dull olive-yellow, with black
wings but no cap. Winter males and juveniles resemble females.

Habitat: Open country, croplands, weedy fields, second-growth
woodlands, and roadsides. Visits bird feeders.

Voice: The goldfinch has a distinctive year-round flight call that
sounds like *per-chik-or-ree*. Males give high-pitched canary-like
songs early in the spring and late in the summer during nesting. Early songs are
rambling and continuous; during nesting they are short and precise, somewhat resembling the songs of Indigo Buntings. A common call is a nasal, ascending *su-weet*
that signals agitation or conflict with another goldfinch. Around the nest, both
sexes give a special *bay-bee* alarm call. Fledglings give a distinctive, peeping *chip-ee,
chip-ee, chip-ee,* as they beg for attention.

Range: Year-round resident across most of the northern half of the United States.
Summer range extends across southern Canada. Winters from the southern states
into Mexico.

28

Eastern Towhee
Pipilo erythrophthalmus

The handsome Eastern Towhee (8″ long) is a skulking species, foraging on the ground for insects and spiders using a distinctive behavior—hopping backward and raking with both feet to stir up the leaf litter where small creatures hide. Towhees also eat seeds and berries. In spring, males claim territories by singing from concealed perches, alternating songs with neighboring rivals. Courtship includes male and female displaying with tails and wings outspread, showing off their white markings. The female towhee secretively builds the nest on the ground, and during incubation she is reluctant to fly if disturbed. Both adults feed the young. In winter, towhees gather in small flocks, often with cardinals, sparrows, and juncos.

Identification: The adult male has a black hood and back, white belly, bold white wing patches and tail corners, and distinctive reddish brown flanks. The adult female is similar but brown where male is black. Immatures are streaked brown, but with the adult wing and tail pattern.

Habitat: Open woodlands with dense undergrowth, brushy forest edges, streamside thickets.

Voice: The male's typical song consists of two short notes followed by a higher-pitched trill, often paraphrased as *drink-your-teeeeeeeee.* Simpler songs may also be heard. The commonly heard call is a loud, ringing *che-wink* or *ta-weee,* given by both sexes as a contact call, and also in alarm. Towhees also make high *chips.*

Range: Year-round resident throughout much of the eastern United States, except for northern and midwestern areas where it is a summer resident only. Winters in the south-central states.

29

Eastern Meadowlark
Sturnella magna

With a plaintive, flutelike song, the male Eastern Meadowlark (9″ long) proclaims ownership of his grassland home from an exposed perch, often a fence post or telephone pole. In spring, territorial meadowlarks perform flight displays, jumping into the air and fluttering down to the ground with wings elevated. During aggressive encounters they display to rivals by fluffing out their plumage and pointing their bills upward. The female often answers the song of her mate with a sputtering call. She builds the nest, with a dome of grasses woven above it, on the ground. Males are often polygynous, with two or more females nesting on their territories. The Eastern Meadowlark is remarkably similar in appearance to the Western Meadowlark (a western species), but the two can be distinguished by sound.

Identification: Adults of both sexes have streaked brown upperparts, bright yellow underparts, and a bold, black V-shaped bar across their breasts. White outer tail feathers are distinctive in flight.

Habitat: Found in hayfields, meadows, and prairies.

Voice: The male's song is a series of two to eight clear, whistled notes, some slurred together, and often sounding like *seee-yeee, seee-yer.* A popular memory phrase for the song is *spring-o-the-year.* The female often responds with a chattering sputter, especially during courtship. A short, buzzy *dzert* is given when meadowlarks are alarmed or during territorial encounters.

Range: Year-round resident across much of the eastern United States, parts of the Southwest, and into Central America. Summer breeding range extends into southeastern Canada.

30

Brown-headed Cowbird
Molothrus ater

The Brown-headed Cowbird (7″ long) is renowned for its habit of nest parasitism. It lays eggs in the nests of other bird species, especially warblers, vireos, and sparrows, which then incubate and raise the young cowbirds at the expense of their own reproductive success. In spring, small flocks of males perform noisy courtship displays to females, fluffing out their feathers, spreading wings and tail, and toppling forward while singing. Females mate with the dominant male in a courting group and then secretively invade the nests of hosts. One egg is laid in each nest, the resulting fledgling sometimes being much larger than its foster parents. Cowbirds often forage among herds of grazing farm animals, feeding on insects that are scared up—this is how the cowbird earned its name.

female

Identification: Adult male is glossy black with a brown head. Adult female is brownish gray overall. Both have dark gray conical bills. Immatures resemble adult females.

Habitat: Agricultural fields, pastures, woodland edges, suburbs.

Voice: The male's song consists of several faint bubbling sounds followed by a long squeak, *bublo-seeleeee,* given as the male topples forward. Females give a rapid series of liquid chattering sounds, often when the male sings. Upon taking flight, males commonly give a squeaky three-note whistle: *pseeee-see-see.*

Range: Year-round resident across much of eastern United States, the Southwest, and the West Coast. Summer range extends into Canada. Population is increasing because forest fragmentation exposes more bird species to cowbird parasitism.

31

Canada Goose
Branta canadensis

The familiar Canada Goose is strongly monogamous, with paired birds remaining together as long as both live. It varies from 25″–45″ long, depending on the region, northern birds being the largest. Highly territorial while breeding, Canada Geese communicate vocally and by means of head and neck postures. Hissing with head lowered and neck coiled or outstretched signifies threat. Pumping the head up and down warns of attack. Upright neck and head wagging means alarm. Members of a pair often perform a noisy, elaborate greeting ritual—with neck outstretched, the male rolls his head vigorously from side to side, giving snorelike calls, then both birds give a duet of excited honks. Breeds in wetlands, where the nest is often placed on an abandoned muskrat house.

Identification: Adults of both sexes are brownish gray with black head and neck and a broad white chinstrap.

Habitat: Feeds in water on submerged vegetation. Also grazes on grasses and winter wheat and is often seen in fields feeding on waste corn. Breeds in protected ponds, lakes, and marshes.

Voice: Most often heard is a musical honking as migrating flocks fly overhead. The male's call is a low *a-honk,* the female's a higher *hink* or *a-hink.* A pair may alternate their honks so closely that it sounds like a single bird: *a-hink-a-honk-a-hink-a-honk.* Other sounds include aggressive barks and hisses. Young make wavering whistles.

Range: Year-round resident across most of the United States and along the west coast of Canada. Summer range extends throughout Canada and Alaska. Winters across the southern states into Mexico.

32

Mallard
Anas platyrhynchos

The Mallard (22″ long) is one of our best-known native ducks. A "dabbling" duck, it gathers food on the water's surface or up-ends itself to thrust its bill underwater to feed on aquatic plants or small water creatures. Courtship takes place in fall and winter, with mallards forming groups in which both sexes perform a variety of distinctive displays. Courting males give soft grunts and whistles as they arch their necks upward and throw droplets of water into the air. A female may swim after a male and display by repeatedly flicking her bill back over one side of her body. Both sexes may be seen swimming to and fro rapidly, with necks outstretched and heads just above the water's surface. Mallards nest on the ground, near water.

female

Identification: The male Mallard has a silver-gray body, with an iridescent green head and neck separated from a chestnut breast by a fine white neck band. The female is heavily streaked brown and has an orange bill marked with black patches. Both sexes have blue wing patches, sometimes not visible.

Habitat: Ponds, lakes, rivers, parks, marshes.

Voice: The Mallard's typical quacking is given only by the female; it is often heard during the nesting season. When courted by males in the fall, females respond with loud quacks that decrease in volume and pitch: *k-QUACK-Quack-quack-quack*. Courting females also make a froglike cackle. The common call of the male is a soft, nasal *rhaeb-rhaeb*. Males also make grunting whistles during courtship.

Range: Year-round resident across much of the United States, except for the southernmost states, which are wintering areas. Summers in subarctic Canada and Alaska.

33

Wood Duck
Aix sponsa

Perhaps our most beautiful native duck, the multicolored, crested Wood Duck (18″ long) is unforgettable. Courtship begins in the autumn, with groups of males performing elaborate displays to females. Pair formation occurs in midwinter. Wood Ducks inhabit wooded swamps and nest in natural tree cavities and artificial nest boxes. Prior to nesting, a female investigates potential nest holes while her mate perches nearby. Young leave the nest by jumping to the ground or water and following the female to a feeding area. Wood Ducks are our only native perching ducks; they may often be seen resting on tree limbs above water.

female

Identification: The breeding male, with his sleeked-down crest, has an iridescent green-purple head with red eyes and bill and a brown, cream, and blue body, with bold black and white markings throughout. The female is overall brownish gray, with a prominent white eye-ring and blue wing patch. Males in "eclipse" plumage, after the summer molt, resemble females, but retain their distinctive facial pattern. Young birds resemble the female, but have more spotting on their underparts.

Habitat: Wooded swampy areas, lakes, rivers, and ponds with woods nearby.

Voice: The most familiar Wood Duck call is a nasal *ooo-eek, ooo-eek,* given by the female in flight or while swimming. Males in courtship groups perform head-flicking and other displays accompanied by rising, buzzy whistles: *jeeee-ib.* Females searching for nest sites make a soft, stuttering *oo-oo-oo-oo-ah-ah.*

Range: Summers throughout much of eastern North America and in the Northwest. Year-round resident in southeastern states and along the West Coast.

34

Great Blue Heron
Ardea herodias

A tall, elegant bird, the Great Blue Heron (about 48″ long) is our largest and most widespread heron. Cautiously stalking through shallow water or waiting motionless for prey to come within reach, it captures a variety of fish, frogs, birds, aquatic insects, and small mammals. Great Blue Herons nest in small colonies, building stick platforms at the tops of tall trees in forests or in shrubs on secluded islands (where they occasionally nest on the ground if there are no predators). At the nest, a spectacular courtship display occurs in which the male and female point their bills skyward and spread out their neck plumes. Courting birds may also lock the tips of their bills and sway to and fro. Territorial displays involve raising crest and neck feathers while bill clapping. In wintering areas, Great Blues join communal roosts with other species of herons.

Identification: Adults of both sexes are gray-blue, with a whitish head and a broad black stripe above the eye. Breeding birds have long plumes on the head, neck, and back. Immatures lack the plumes and have a solid black cap.

Habitat: Frequents lake and river edges, swamps, freshwater and salt marshes, and tidal flats. Nesting colonies are sometimes far removed from aquatic feeding areas.

Voice: A harsh guttural *rok-rok,* or a drawn-out croaking *frahnk* are given during aggressive interactions, when alarmed, or when taking flight. Sounds at the breeding colony include the staccato *kek-kek-kek-kek-kek* of begging young and the raspy, gagging calls and croaks of adults.

Range: Year-round resident across most of the United States and along the west coast of Canada to Alaska. Summers from the upper Midwest into Canada.

35

Belted Kingfisher
Ceryle alcyon

The Belted Kingfisher (13″ long) is a widespread and conspicuous species that frequents diverse aquatic habitats. It perches, or sometimes hovers, above open water and plunge-dives for small fish, crayfish, and other aquatic creatures. While perched, a kingfisher frequently bobs its head and tail and raises its crest. The nest is at the end of a tunnel in a dirt or sand bank, which the mates excavate by digging with their bills and then kicking out loosened soil with their feet. Nests are often located in old quarries or along roads, far from wetland feeding areas. In winter, kingfishers remain in northern areas as long as ice-free water remains.

Identification: A chunky, compact bird with a large head, a long, pointed bill, shaggy crest, and short legs and tail. Both sexes are blue-gray above and white below, with a blue-gray breast band. Females have an additional rust-colored breast band. Juveniles resemble adults but have brown feathers in their gray breast bands.

Habitat: Wetlands, including lakes, ponds, rivers, streams, and estuaries.

Voice: The major call is a strident rattle, varying in loudness and intensity depending on the bird's circumstances. A loud, long sequence indicates excitement or alarm, while a shorter, softer volley may be used as a contact call between mates. Kingfishers are intensely territorial and call regularly in flight as they patrol streams or shorelines. In aggressive interactions the rattle call is especially harsh. The nestling call is a throaty warble, which becomes more rattlelike as the young mature.

Range: Year-round resident across much of the continental United States. The summer range extends to northern Canada and Alaska. Northernmost breeders migrate south, some traveling as far as northern South America.

36

Tree Swallow
Tachycineta bicolor

Gregarious in lifestyle and graceful in flight, Tree Swallows (6″ long) often gather over water, swooping to snatch insects from the air. They nest in natural tree cavities and nest boxes, often occupying boxes intended for bluebirds. When courting, the male hovers or flutters near the perched female. At their nest site, the pair performs a bowing display, accompanied by vocalizing and bill touching. The nest of grasses is lined with many feathers. When cool weather reduces insect activity, Tree Swallows sometimes disappear from their breeding area for several days, only to return and resume nesting. Outside the breeding season, Tree Swallows gather in huge flocks and roost in marshy areas.

Identification: Adult males are glossy blue-green above and white below. Females are similar, but, depending on their age, may have browner foreheads and backs. One-year-old males have adult male coloration, but one-year-old females have brownish upperparts, becoming glossy blue-green with successive molts.

Habitat: Wooded habitats near water and wetlands flooded by beavers. Also frequents open fields and meadows, especially where nest boxes are provided.

Voice: The male sings a long-continued, twittery "dawn song" in flight or from a perch: *teet, trrit, teet, teet, trrit, teet, trrit.* Typical daytime song, given mostly by the male, is a short series of high notes followed by a gurgling jumble. The alarm call is a sharp *chee-deep* or *chiddy-deep.* Various raspy calls are given during interactions.

Range: Summers throughout most of the United States (excluding southern areas), and much of Canada and Alaska. Winters in Florida, along the Gulf Coast, and into Mexico and Central America.

37

Marsh Wren
Cistothorus palustris

The tiny, energetic Marsh Wren (5″ long) inhabits dense cat-tails and bulrushes in freshwater and brackish marshes through-out North America. The male may have several mates, each in-habiting a different nest on his territory. In spring, he sings throughout the day and often at night, and he displays by flying up into the air and then softly fluttering down onto another part of his territory. He builds a number of unlined nests, which reduce predation on occupied nests by acting as decoys. Nests are globular and have a side entrance. They are woven of reeds and cattails placed a foot or so above water level. Courtship displays include the male Marsh Wren fluffing his plumage, leaning down with his tail cocked over his back, and swaying to and fro at the female. She chooses one of his many nests and adds a lining of cattail fluff before laying her eggs.

Identification: The sexes look alike: stumpy little brown birds with slender bills, barred plumage, and upturned tails. A striped back, solid brown crown, and bold white eyebrow stripe set this species apart from other wrens.

Habitat: Freshwater and brackish marshes, especially among cattail and bulrush.

Voice: The male's song is a series of reedy, gurgling warbles followed by a dry, rattling trill. Individual males have many song patterns, ranging from about 40 in eastern populations to nearly 150 in some western regions. Calls include a dry *chek,* a rattling *churrrr,* and various whimpering notes.

Range: Resident year-round along much of the East Coast and Gulf Coast of the United States, and in the West. Summers in the northern half of the United States and southern Canada. Winter range includes the south-central states and Mexico.

38

Common Yellowthroat
Geothlypis trichas

The Common Yellowthroat (5″ long) is a widespread, abundant species that frequents moist shrubby thickets, wet grassy areas with bushes, and marshes with thick cattails and reeds. The yellowthroat is the only member of the "wood warbler" family that nests in open, marshy habitats. Yellowthroats are skulking birds, gleaning insect food from vegetation. The well-concealed nest, built by the female, is found close to the ground. Nests are often parasitized by Brown-headed Cowbirds.

Identification: Both sexes have olive-brown upperparts, pale underparts, and yellow under the tail. The male is easily recognized by his prominent bright yellow throat and black facial mask. Females lack the mask but have a yellow throat. Young birds resemble the female.

Habitat: Yellowthroats frequent a variety of open or brushy habitats, ranging from overgrown fields and hedgerows to the shrubby edges of marshes and swamps.

Voice: The male's distinctive, high-pitched song is a series of repeated phrases: *witchety-witchety-witchety-witch.* The song is loud for such a small bird, and the singer rarely stays put, hopping or flying from perch to perch between songs. The male also performs a special "flight song," given as he rises high into the air on fluttering wings. It begins with high *tink* notes followed by two loud *chips,* then several typical song phrases, and finally a complex jumble of notes as the bird descends. The distinctive alarm call is a rattling *tschat* or sharp *steek.* During aggressive social encounters, yellowthroats often make a chattering rattle.

Range: Summers throughout most of North America, excluding the Far North. Year-round resident in the southeastern states and Mexico.

39

Red-winged Blackbird
Agelaius phoeniceus

In spring, the ringing voices and bright colors of Red-winged Blackbirds (8″ long) enliven freshwater marshes and meadows, where they form loose breeding colonies. Each territorial male sings from a perch, often a cattail seedhead, and performs a dramatic courtship display, spreading his wings and tail and flaring out his scarlet shoulder patches as he sings. At the height of courtship, groups of males engage in rapid chases of females, each male then returning to his own territory to resume displaying. Males may have more than one mate. Females build cup-shaped nests suspended from cattails or other vegetation, often over water. In fall and winter, Red-wings form large flocks and forage in wetlands and crop fields.

female

Identification: Male is overall jet black with scarlet shoulder patches bordered by yellow. Female is heavily streaked dark brown overall. Juveniles resemble adult females, and young males have an orange shoulder patch.

Habitat: Breeds in freshwater marshes, shrub swamps, and upland hayfields. Forages in fields and other open areas.

Voice: The male's song is a loud, gurgling *conk-la-reeeeee* or *o-ka-leeeee*. The female's primary call is a sputtering chatter, often given just as her mate sings; it is considered by some to be female song. The basic alarm or contact call given by both sexes is a staccato *tsk* or *tink*. Males respond to predators on their territories with a plaintive, whistled *seeeeeee* or *seee-yeee*.

Range: Year-round resident throughout the United States (except northernmost regions) and Mexico. Summers across subarctic Canada.

40

Ruffed Grouse
Bonasa umbellus

A plump, ground-dwelling woodland bird, the Ruffed Grouse (16″–19″ long) has a fascinating nonvocal method of producing sound. The male's "territorial drumming," usually given from a mossy log, is made as the male rapidly beats his stiff wings while standing in an upright position. Each time he pulls his wings apart, a vacuum is created and suddenly broken, creating a rapid series of low-pitched thumps. In spring, his drumming resonates through the forest and attracts females, to whom the male then displays by strutting with fanned tail and raised ruff. After mating, the female nests and raises the young alone. Ruffed Grouse feed on seeds, insects, berries, and buds. In winter, aspen buds are a favorite staple.

Identification: A reddish brown or grayish brown chickenlike bird, whose tail has a broad black band near the tip. The sexes are identical. Two color types are recognized, which are told apart most obviously by tail color—in the southern part of the range these grouse have rufous tails, whereas northern birds have gray tails.

Habitat: Deciduous and mixed woodlands.

Voice: The wing-drumming of the male resembles the deep sound of a distant one-cylinder engine starting up. His thumping is ventriloquial, often making the male difficult to find. The muffled thumps start slowly and then accelerate into a rapid whir: *wup . . . wup . . . wup . . . wup-wup-wup-wurrrrrrrrrrr.* The vocal alarm call is a sputtery *quit-quit-quit-quit-quit.* When disturbed near the nest or with fledglings, the female gives mournful squeals along with a "crippled-bird" distraction display that draws predators in her direction.

Range: Year-round resident across the northern United States, Canada, and Alaska.

41

Wild Turkey
Meleagris gallopavo

Our largest game bird, the Wild Turkey (36″–49″ long) has been successfully reintroduced into much of its original range, after overhunting and habitat loss drastically reduced its numbers in the last century. Turkeys usually forage on the ground in open woodlands for seeds, berries, nuts, acorns, and insects. Wary and with excellent vision, turkeys usually escape danger by running. They are weak fliers, but take to the trees to roost. Turkeys winter in flocks, often feeding on waste grain in fields. During spring courtship, the male's loud gobble is a familiar sound throughout its range. When he encounters a female, the male struts with puffed plumage, fanned tail, and expanded head wattles. Given the opportunity, males mate with many females, which then nest and raise their young alone.

Identification: A large ground-dwelling bird with iridescent brown plumage, and a pink-and-blue bare-skinned head. Males are larger and more iridescent than females and immatures, with fleshy red head wattles and a dark tuft of beardlike feathers on the breast that can be a foot long (females sometimes have short beards).

Habitat: Open woodlands, forest edges, wooded swamps, agricultural areas, and a variety of arid habitats in the Southwest.

Voice: On early spring mornings, the male gives loud gobbling calls that may be heard up to a mile away. Displaying males drag their wings on the ground and make soft, low-pitched moans. Females give yelping calls and various clucking sounds in response. The common alarm call given by females when young are threatened sounds like: *put, put, put, put, put, put . . .*

Range: Year-round, but patchy, resident across the United States; most abundant in eastern and south-central states and some areas of the Northwest.

42

Barred Owl
Strix varia

One of our most vocal owls, the Barred Owl (21″ long) may be heard calling in the day, although its habits are primarily nocturnal. Its vocal repertoire includes otherworldly shrieks as well as typical hoots, and the sound of two individuals interacting is unforgettable. Hoots are easily imitated, and owls can sometimes be attracted for an intimate view. The Barred Owl frequents thick forests and wooded swamps, feeding on rodents, frogs, reptiles, and crayfish. The preferred nest site is a tree cavity, but Barred Owls readily accept nest boxes if the entrance hole is large enough. They will also use abandoned hawk or crow nests.

Identification: A chunky owl with a rounded head, whose dark eyes and lack of ear tufts distinguish it from other large owls. Plumage is gray-brown, distinctively barred across the chest and streaked lengthwise down the belly. The sexes look identical.

Habitat: Coniferous and mixed forests, wooded river bottomlands, and wooded swamps. Very common in swampy woodlands of the Southeast.

Voice: The Barred Owl is famous for its distinctive hooted call series, paraphrased as *"Who cooks for you . . . who cooks for you-all,"* usually with a southern drawl at the end. This hoot pattern is given by both sexes and may function as a contact call or a territorial challenge. Other calls include a series of ascending hoots and a simple, descending *whoo-ahhh.* When two owls meet one another in the darkness, they often hoot back and forth excitedly, alternating and overlapping monkeylike calls in a distinctive manner. Fledglings beg for food with harsh, raspy screeches.

Range: Year-round resident throughout the eastern United States, across much of southern Canada, and into the Northwest.

43

Great Horned Owl
Bubo virginianus

The most widespread North American owl, the Great Horned Owl (22″ long) is a fearsome nocturnal predator, eating mammals ranging in size from tiny mice to squirrels, skunks, and domestic cats. Also eats birds, including smaller owls and hawks. Its earlike "horns" are actually tufts of feathers. Great Horned Owls are among the earliest species to breed. Northern populations lay their eggs well before snow disappears, ensuring that the young owls hatch just as rodents are emerging in spring. The nest is usually in an old hawk nest or tree hollow.

Identification: A large bulky owl, strongly barred with gray, brown, and black. Has widely spaced ear tufts, yellow eyes, and a white throat. If ear tufts are laid back, they may not be clearly visible from a distance. Male and female look alike.

Habitat: Frequents a variety of habitats, including northern forests, southern deserts, rural and agricultural areas, suburbs, and city parks.

Voice: The major call is a series of five or more deep, resonant hoots, all on one pitch: *hoo, hoohoo, hoooo, hoooo,* most commonly given by the male as a territorial advertisement starting in late winter. The pattern of hoots varies among individual males, and several may respond to each other as they call from neighboring territories at dusk or in the predawn hours. Female hoots are higher pitched. Sharp, barking calls are given when the birds are alarmed near the nest. Calls of fledglings and immatures vary from hoarse or raspy screeches to piercing whistles—hair-raising calls that account for most of the "mystery screeches" heard in the dark of the night.

Range: Year-round resident throughout the North American continent, except for the arctic region.

44

Pileated Woodpecker
Dryocopus pileatus

The striking Pileated Woodpecker (18″ long), our biggest wood-pecker, needs a large territory with mature trees in which to nest and feed. Primarily a rural bird, it is increasing in suburbs with large shade trees. In late winter, unmated males start drum-ming to advertise for mates. During courtship, both members of the pair drum and perform bill-waving displays. Territorial and alarm behavior includes wing flicking and crest raising. The nest cavity is excavated in dead wood, mostly by the male. Pileateds channel out long rectangular feeding holes in rotten trees or stumps as they search for carpenter ants, their main winter food.

Identification: Crow-sized black woodpecker with bold white facial markings and a bright red crest. In flight, white wing linings are visible. Male has a red mustache, female's is black. The Pileated Woodpecker is our largest native woodpecker, exclud-ing the probably-extinct Ivory-billed Woodpecker, which is similar in appearance but has large white wing patches.

Habitat: Prefers dense, mature forest, but becoming common in suburbs and sec-ondary-growth woodlands, especially in the South. Comes to suet feeders.

Voice: The distinctive "short call" is a whinnylike outburst of notes that drop in volume and pitch at the end. Another common call is a long series of clucking notes, delivered at a variable rate: *cuk, cuk . . . cuk . . . cuk . . . cuk, cuk . . .* During courtship and territorial encounters, birds often produce a squealing *awoik, awoik, awoik.* Drumming, which is usually quite loud and resonant, is lower in pitch than that of smaller woodpeckers and trails off in volume at the end.

Range: Year-round resident throughout the eastern United States, across much of subarctic Canada, and along the West Coast.

Wood Thrush
Hylocichla mustelina

Drifting lazily through the forest, the haunting, liquid melody of the Wood Thrush (8″ long) is one of summer's joys. The male returns to claim the same breeding territory year after year, singing from prominent perches, mostly at dawn and dusk. Males often alternate their beautiful songs as if performing a musical concert. They threaten intruders by displaying with raised crest or fluffed-out body feathers, and by chases. When a female first arrives, the male sings loudly and at first chases her, but she persists. Soon he begins gathering nest material and the pair visits potential nest sites together. The female builds the nest on a forked tree limb. She also does the incubating, although both parents feed the young.

Identification: Adults of both sexes are rusty brown above, brightest on head and nape and becoming more olive-brown on the rump and tail. Underparts are whitish, with bold dark spots.

Habitat: Moist deciduous or mixed woods, swamps, and suburbs with woodlots.

Voice: The male's song begins with several soft, almost inaudible notes followed by a beautiful sequence of flutelike whistles that rise and fall in pitch and usually end with a high, liquid trill: *tut, tut, oh-lay-oh-leeeee.* Each male has a repertoire of several different song types. Neighboring males may sing back and forth with such precision that they are mistaken for a single bird singing. Calls range from short volleys of soft, throaty notes *(bup-bup-bup-bup),* to excited, whinnylike outbursts of high-pitched, liquid notes *(pit-pit-pit-pit-pit-pit-pit).*

Range: Summer visitor only, breeding throughout the eastern half of the United States, excluding Florida, and into southeastern Canada. Winters in Central America.

46

Rose-breasted Grosbeak
Pheucticus ludovicianus

A strikingly handsome, chunky songbird, the Rose-breasted Grosbeak (8″ long) whistles a song often described as "a robin in a hurry." The male's brilliant, rose-red breast patch varies in size and shape among individuals, allowing observers to tell one male from another. During courtship the male performs a flight display with outspread tail and shallow wingbeats, showing off his white wing patches and giving a rapid version of the song. Male and female share incubation and feeding of the young.

female

Identification: Male in breeding plumage has black upperparts, a white belly with a pinkish red triangular breast patch, and white rump and wing patches. Winter male has buff edges to the black feathers. The gray-brown female, resembling a large chunky sparrow, has a white eyebrow and heavy brown streaking on her whitish breast. Immature males resemble the female, but have a rosy breast patch.

Habitat: Deciduous woodlands, residential woodlots, orchards, and thickets. Visits backyard bird feeders for sunflower seed.

Voice: Song is a sequence of rich, slurred whistles, similar to the American Robin's, but hurried in comparison and perhaps more musical in quality. Females may give shortened versions of songs near the nest. The most familiar call is a brief metallic *chink*. Nasal *weep* and *eeee* calls are given by birds in social situations. Fledglings give distinctive, vibrant begging calls: *teee-yooo*.

Range: Summer visitor, breeding in the northeastern and north-central United States and central Canada. Winters in Central America.

47

Red-eyed Vireo
Vireo olivaceus

In spring, the male Red-eyed Vireo (6″ long) spends most of his time proclaiming his territoriality by singing constantly high in the treetops. Vireos are difficult to see among the leaves; it is the monotonous and persistent singing that alerts us to a bird's presence. The female alone builds the nest, a beautiful structure of birch bark strips, plant-stem fibers, paper from wasp nests, and spider egg cases, bound together with spider or caterpillar webs and hung from a forked tree branch in the forest understory. During nesting, the male's rate of singing increases. He stops singing only for brief periods to interact with his mate, bringing her food while she incubates on the nest or perches nearby. Red-eyed Vireos are common hosts of the parasitic Brown-headed Cowbird.

Identification: Adults of both sexes are dark olive green above with whitish underparts. Distinctive are the blue-gray cap and the white eyebrow, bordered on either side with black. The iris of the eye is ruby red in adults and brown in immatures, but this characteristic is difficult to see at a distance.

Habitat: Deciduous and mixed woodlands, rural areas, and suburbs with woodlots.

Voice: The male's song is an extended series of short whistled phrases, each slightly different; they are separated by brief pauses: *sewee, seewit, seeowit, seeyee.* Song rate is about 40 phrases per minute early in spring and faster during incubation. Males sing all day long—one researcher followed an individual and counted over 20,000 songs in a single day! The common alarm call is a nasal *chway* or *nyaah.*

Range: A summer visitor only, breeding throughout the United States (excluding the Southwest) and across much of subarctic Canada.

48

Yellow-rumped Warbler
Dendroica coronata

One of the most abundant American warblers is the Yellow-rumped Warbler (5½″ long), formerly considered two species: the "Myrtle Warbler" in the North and East and the "Audubon's Warbler" in the West. Commonly seen flitting through trees and shrubs in search of insects, Yellow-rumps also forage low to the ground and over water, particularly during migration. Their diet includes berries, enabling Yellow-rumps to be one of the last warbler species to migrate south. During courtship, singing males raise their yellow crown feathers. For nesting, the birds choose a horizontal branch high in a coniferous tree. The nest is a deep cup of small twigs, bark strips, and plant fibers, with a lining of grasses into which feathers are woven, their tips curving over to shelter the eggs.

Identification: The distinctive yellow rump and yellow patches in front of each wing are present in all plumages. Spring "Myrtle" males have a yellow crown patch and a white throat; "Audubon's" males have a yellow throat. Spring females, fall adults, and juveniles are browner and duller than breeding males.

Habitat: Breeds in coniferous and mixed forests of the North and West. During migration and winter, Yellow-rumps frequent woodlands and thickets, often gathering in shrubby areas with concentrations of bayberry and wax myrtle.

Voice: The male's song is a high-pitched musical trill with a variable ending. The common call is a dry *check,* often interspersed with song.

Range: The summer breeding range includes the western and far northeastern United States and most of Canada and Alaska. Common winter resident from the East Coast to Texas and Mexico. Year-round resident along the West Coast into Mexico.

49

Scarlet Tanager
Piranga olivacea

Vivid coloration makes the Scarlet Tanager (7″ long) one of our most beautiful birds, a veritable "flame of spring" that brightens the woodland green. Found in the forest canopy, tanagers are best located by their burry songs. Their need for large forest patches in which to breed makes them particularly vulnerable to deforestation. The flimsy nest, built by the female, is found high above the ground, out on a horizontal branch. The female incubates alone and is fed by the male, at or near the nest.

Identification: Male in breeding plumage is bright red with black wings and tail. Female has olive upperparts, slightly darker wings and tail, and yellowish underparts. Molting males have blotches of red and olive, and male winter plumage resembles the female, but with black wings.

Habitat: Breeds in mature deciduous forests, particularly oak woodlands. Also found in parks, orchards, and suburban areas with large trees and woodlots.

Voice: The male's song is a sequence of buzzy, robinlike phrases: *queer, queerit, queereo, queer,* given with long pauses between songs. The song is often described as sounding like "a robin with a sore throat." At dawn, males sing more continuously, interspersing calls with songs. Females may also sing, particularly while gathering nest material or food—their songs are usually softer and shorter than those of males. The most commonly heard call sounds like *chick-breee* or *chip-burrr.* It is given by both sexes during territorial disputes or in the presence of danger, usually accompanied by drooping wings and flicking tail.

Range: Summer visitor only, breeding from southeastern Canada to the southeastern United States. Winters in northern South America.

50

Dark-eyed Junco
Junco hyemalis

The Dark-eyed Junco (6″ long) is the familiar "snowbird" that visits our bird feeders in winter, but heads north to forested habitat to nest in spring. Several variants exist, including the "Slate-colored" in the East, the "Oregon," "Pink-sided," and "Gray-headed" in the West, and the "White-winged" in the north-central states. Winter flocks have fixed social hierarchies. Dominant juncos displace underlings by charging and pecking at them. Another aggressive stance involves fanned tail, raised wings, and open bill. Two juncos, face to face, may bob their heads up and down, especially during aggressive or sexual encounters. In spring, males trill their ringing songs from atop trees. The nest is built on the ground, well hidden against a rocky outcrop, exposed soil bank, or the root system of a fallen tree. Juncos often nest along hiking trails in mixed or coniferous forest.

Identification: "Slate-colored" adult male (shown) is dark gray with white belly; the female is browner than the male (for descriptions of other forms, consult a comprehensive field guide). All juncos have conspicuous white outer tail feathers.

Habitat: Breeding habitat includes coniferous and mixed forests, woodland edges, bogs, and mountainous regions. Winters in woodland edges and brushy areas. Common winter visitor to backyard bird feeders.

Voice: Male's song is a simple musical trill, sometimes likened to the sound of a ringing telephone. Calls include a nasal *kew-kew-kew-kew* and a buzzy *zeet,* given during social interactions, and a smacking *tick,* given when the nest is threatened.

Range: Year-round resident in northeastern and western United States. Summer range includes much of Canada and Alaska. Winters over much of the United States.

Where to Go from Here

We hope that this introduction to 50 of North America's avian favorites will encourage you to step further into the fascinating world of birds. Bird watching is both fun and challenging, and there's room for all levels of interest and ability. If you're wondering what you should do next, we recommend the following:

Purchase a comprehensive field identification guide to birds. Whether you plan to start a life list or are more interested in studying bird behavior, you'll need to know exactly which of North America's more than 800 breeding species you are watching. There are many excellent field guides on the market, including the popular Peterson Field Guides published by Houghton Mifflin Company.

Buy the best binoculars you can afford. Technical advice is beyond our scope here, but remember that both light-gathering ability and magnification are important considerations. Ask birding friends for recommendations, read product reviews, and be sure to try out binoculars before you buy. And don't forget—always take your binoculars with you when you travel.

Subscribe to a birding magazine. Several good ones are available, with topics ranging from bird natural history, behavior, and conservation issues, to birding hotspots, birding techniques, identification tips, and bird photography. Visit your local library or bookstore and read books about birds and birding. Subjects are as varied as the birds themselves—look for bird encyclopedias, regional guides to birding hotspots, introductions to bird behavior, and books that cover specific groups of birds, such as owls, hawks, shorebirds, songbirds, waterfowl, and warblers.

Join a local birding club, nature association, or National Audubon Society chapter. There you will meet other birders, learn about local birding spots, and participate in field trips. Visit local nature centers, state parks, and national wildlife refuges—take advantage of their programs about birds and other nature-related topics, and participate in guided walks oriented toward birders.

Finally and most importantly, get out and watch the birds! Bird watching is our favorite pastime—we hope it will become yours too!

Credits and Acknowledgments

The Photographs

All but four of the photographs featured in this book are by Lang Elliott or Marie Read. Lang used a Canon EOS system, and most of his images were captured using a 500mm/f4.5 lens coupled with a 1.4x teleconverter. Marie used Nikon equipment and relied heavily on her 400mm/f3.5 lens coupled with a 1.4x converter. Most images were made using Fuji Velvia (ISO 50) or Fuji Sensia (ISO 100) films. Both authors used photographic blinds to obtain striking close-ups of the birds.

Photograph credits, referenced to page numbers in the book:

Lang Elliott—front cover, 1, 15, 16, 19, 27, 28, 31, 41, 43, 44, 47, 50, 51, 52, 53, 55, 57, 70, 71, 73, 75, 76, 79, 82, 83, 95, 99, 100, 113, 115, 117, 119, 121, 126

Marie Read—2, 4–5, 6, 8, 12–13, 25, 26, 29, 33, 35, 37, 39, 40, 45, 49, 59, 61, 67, 69, 77, 81, 85, 86, 87, 89, 91, 93, 97, 101, 103, 105, 111, 114, 123, back cover

Tom Vezo—63, 65, 109

Steven D. Faccio—107

The Sound Recordings

Most field recordings on the compact disc were made by Lang Elliott, mostly using a portable Sony TCD-D10 Pro DAT recorder and various microphones, including a Sennheiser MKH-20 mounted in a Dan Gibson sound parabola and a Sennheiser MKH-70 shotgun microphone. Additional recordings were provided by the Borror Laboratory of Bioacoustics at Ohio State University, Bill Evans, and Ted Mack.

Acknowledgments

We thank everyone who has helped make this book possible, including John Bower, Kat Dalton, Anne Kilgore, Michael Rider, Peter Wrege, and our editor Harry Foster.

Index to Common Names

Keyed to species numbers which correspond to track numbers on the compact disc.

About the Authors

LANG ELLIOTT is a nature recordist, wildlife photographer, and nature writer. He is the author of a variety of audio guides to wildlife sounds, including the recent *Stokes Field Guide to Bird Songs*. He now designs and packages nature books with audio compact discs, *Common Birds and Their Songs* being his first production. Lang lives in Ithaca, New York.

MARIE READ is an acclaimed wildlife photographer and nature writer whose photographs are featured in many national and international magazines, books, and calendars. Her beautiful images of birds regularly grace the covers of *Birder's World* and *Living Bird* magazines. Originally from England, Marie lives near Ithaca, New York.

 Designed and produced by Lang Elliott, NatureSound Studio, P.O. Box 84, Ithaca, New York 14851-0084. Phone: 607-257-4995. Web site: www.naturesound.com. E-mail: lang@naturesound.com.